# THE ALL I
# PRESE~~RVATION GUIDE~~

*by Miriam Smucker*

## COPYRIGHT© 2010-2025 JKW Enterprises, Inc.  All Rights Reserved:

No part of this material may be reproduced or transmitted in any form whatsoever, electronic, or mechanical, including photocopying, recording, or by any informational storage or retrieval system without express written, dated, and signed permission from the author(s).

## Disclaimer and/or Legal Notices:

While every attempt has been made to verify the information provided in this publication, neither the Author nor the Publisher assumes any responsibility for errors, omissions, or contrary interpretation of the subject matter herein. This publication is not intended for use as a source of legal or accounting advice. The Publisher wants to stress that the information contained herein may be subject to varying state and/or local laws or regulations. All users are advised to retain competent counsel to determine what state and/or local laws or regulations may apply to the user's particular business.

The Purchaser or Reader of this publication assumes responsibility for the use of these materials and information. Adherence to all applicable laws and regulations, federal, state, and local, governing professional licensing, business practices, advertising, and all other aspects of doing business in the United States or any other jurisdiction is the sole responsibility of the Purchaser or Reader. The Author and Publisher assume no responsibility or liability whatsoever on the behalf of any Purchaser or Reader of these materials. Any perceived slights of specific people or organizations are unintentional.

# Table of Contents

# INTRODUCTION

When I was a little girl growing up in a small town in Pennsylvania, the rhythm of the seasons was marked not by the calendar on the wall, but by the work that needed to be done. In the spring, we planted the garden. In the summer, we tended it and began to preserve the early harvest. In the fall, we worked from dawn to dusk, putting up the bounty of the garden and preparing for the long winter ahead. And in the winter, we rested, grateful for the full pantry that would sustain us until the earth warmed again.

Preservation was not a hobby or a trend; it was a way of life. It was how we survived. And it was how we thrived, even in the leanest of times. My mother, my grandmother, and all the women before them were masters of the art of preservation. They knew how to turn a bushel of tomatoes into jars of sauce that would last for years. They knew how to cure a ham so that it would hang in the cellar, safe and delicious, for months on end. And they knew how to render the fat from a hog and use it to preserve meat in crocks that would feed us through the winter.

These were not skills they learned from books. They were skills that were passed down from mother to daughter, from generation to generation, through the simple act of working side by side in the kitchen. I learned to can by standing on a stool next to my mother, watching her carefully pack the jars and seal them with a practiced hand. I learned to cure meat by helping my father in the smokehouse, breathing in the sweet smell of applewood and listening to his quiet instructions. And I learned to render lard by standing next to my grandmother at the stove, stirring the pot and listening to her stories of the old days.

When I left my Amish community in my early twenties, I carried these skills with me. They were a part of who I was, a connection to my roots and to the generations of women who had come before me. But I also carried with me a deep desire to share these skills with others, to help people rediscover the simple, satisfying work of preserving food and the peace of mind that comes from a well-stocked pantry.

Today, I live on a small homestead in rural Ohio, where I continue to practice the old ways. I still can my own vegetables, cure my own bacon, and render my own lard. And I still feel that deep sense of satisfaction that comes from knowing that I can provide for myself and my family, no matter what the future may hold.

In this book, I want to share with you the five essential methods of meat preservation that have sustained my family for generations. These are not fancy, complicated techniques. They are simple, time-tested methods that anyone can learn. Whether you're a seasoned homesteader or a complete beginner, I believe you will find something of value in these pages.

My hope is that as you begin to practice these old ways, you will feel a sense of connection to the past and a sense of empowerment for the future. I hope you will discover the joy of working with your hands, the satisfaction of a job well done, and the peace of mind that comes from knowing you can take care of yourself and your loved ones.

So, let's begin this journey together. Let's roll up our sleeves, tie on our aprons, and rediscover the lost art of meat preservation.

With warm regards,

*Miriam Smucker*

# CHAPTER 1: THE FOUNDATION OF PRESERVATION

It feels like just yesterday I was a little girl, my bare feet cool on the worn wooden floors of our kitchen in a small town in Pennsylvania. My mother, a woman whose hands were never idle, would be at the great wooden table, a mountain of freshly harvested green beans before her. The air would be thick with the smell of dill and vinegar, a scent that for me will always mean summer is ending and the season of putting up has begun.

"Waste not, want not, Miriam," she would say, her voice as steady and comforting as the rhythm of her work. "The good Lord provides for us, and it's our duty to be good stewards of His bounty."

Those long days in the kitchen, watching my mother transform the garden's harvest into rows of gleaming jars that would line our pantry shelves, taught me a lesson that has stayed with me my whole life: true wealth isn't about having a lot of money in the bank, but about having a pantry full of food to feed your family through the lean winter months. It's a feeling of security, of self-reliance, that no supermarket can ever give you.

In this book, I want to share with you the old ways of preserving meat, the ways my mother taught me, and her mother taught her. These are methods that have sustained our people for generations, long before refrigerators and freezers were a part of every home. They are simple, they are effective, and they will give you that same sense of peace and security that I learned as a child.

## THE WHY BEHIND THE HOW

Before we roll up our sleeves and get to the business of canning, curing, and smoking, it's important to understand the **why** behind the **how**. Why do these methods work? The answer is simple: they all fight the same invisible enemies – the bacteria, yeasts, and molds that cause food to spoil.

Think of it like this: these tiny organisms need three things to thrive: water, a comfortable temperature, and the right level of acidity. To preserve meat, we simply have to take away one or more of those things.

- **Salt and Sugar**: These are the workhorses of preservation. They are hygroscopic, which is a fancy way of saying they draw water out of the meat and out of the cells of any bacteria present, effectively killing them.

- **Heat**: This is the principle behind canning. By heating the meat to a high enough temperature for a long enough time, we kill any harmful bacteria and create a vacuum seal in the jar that prevents new bacteria from getting in.

- **Smoke**: The compounds in wood smoke are natural preservatives. They not only add a wonderful flavor to the meat but also have antimicrobial and antioxidant properties that slow down spoilage.

- **Fat**: By submerging meat in fat, as we do in confit, we create an airtight barrier that keeps oxygen and bacteria out.

## THE BOTULISM THREAT: A WORD OF CAUTION

Now, I know some folks get a little nervous when they hear the word "botulism." It's a scary word, and for good reason. Botulism is a rare but serious illness caused by a toxin produced by the bacterium *Clostridium botulinum*. This bacterium is found in the soil and can thrive in low-oxygen, low-acid, and moist environments – exactly the conditions that can be created in a canning jar if you're not careful.

But here's the thing: botulism is entirely preventable. The key is to follow the rules and never take shortcuts. The two most important rules are:

1. For low-acid foods like meat, you MUST use a pressure canner. A water bath canner does not get hot enough to kill botulism spores.

2. Follow tested recipes and processing times. Don't guess or assume. The times and temperatures in this book have been proven to be safe.

Don't let fear keep you from the rewarding work of preserving your own food. With a little knowledge and a healthy dose of respect for the process, you can safely and confidently fill your pantry with delicious, home-preserved meats.

## THE $0.37 INGREDIENT: THE POWER OF SALT

If there's one ingredient that is the cornerstone of nearly all meat preservation, it's salt. It's so common, so inexpensive, that we often take it for granted. But in the world of preservation, salt is king.

For centuries, salt was the primary means of preserving meat. It was so valuable that Roman soldiers were sometimes paid in salt – which is where the word "salary" comes from.

Salt works its magic in two ways. First, as we've already discussed, it draws water out of the meat, making it an inhospitable environment for bacteria. Second, it penetrates the muscle fibers, adding flavor and helping to tenderize the meat.

We'll talk more about the different kinds of salt and how to use them in the chapters on curing and smoking, but for now, just remember that this humble, everyday ingredient is the key to unlocking a world of delicious, long-lasting preserved meats.

## THE "CONTROLLED DECAY" PRINCIPLE

When we talk about curing meat, what we're really talking about is a process of "controlled decay." I know that sounds a little unsettling, but it's the best way to describe what's happening.

When you pack a piece of meat in salt and spices, you're not just preventing spoilage; you're also encouraging the growth of beneficial bacteria that transform the meat, giving it a deeper, more complex flavor and a tender texture. It's the same principle that's at work when you make cheese or wine.

This is the art of curing: creating the perfect conditions for the good bacteria to thrive while keeping the bad bacteria at bay. It's a dance between salt, temperature, and time, and when you get it right, the results are nothing short of miraculous.

Now that we've laid the foundation, let's get to the heart of the matter. In the next chapter, we'll start with the most modern and versatile of all the preservation methods: pressure canning. It's the workhorse of the Amish kitchen, and it will soon be the workhorse of yours, too.

## RECIPE: CANNED GROUND BEEF OR SAUSAGE

Having jars of pre-cooked ground beef or sausage on the shelf is a true time-saver. It's like having a meal halfway made! You can use it in chili, spaghetti sauce, tacos, or any recipe that calls for browned ground meat. I always make a big batch of this in the fall, after we've processed our beef for the year. It's a comfort to know that even on a busy night, a hearty meal is just a jar away.

**Ingredients:**

- Lean ground beef or pork sausage (at least 80% lean)

- Canning salt (optional)

**Instructions:**

1. Shape the ground meat into patties or crumble it into a large skillet. Cook until about two-thirds done, stirring occasionally. Do not brown it completely, as it will finish cooking in the canner.
2. Drain off all the fat. This is very important for a safe seal.
3. Pack the hot meat loosely into hot pint or quart jars, leaving 1-inch headspace.
4. Add ½ teaspoon of canning salt to each pint jar or 1 teaspoon to each quart jar, if desired.
5. Pour boiling water, tomato juice, or meat broth over the meat, leaving 1-inch headspace.
6. Remove air bubbles, wipe the jar rims, and adjust the two-piece caps.
7. Process in a pressure canner according to the times listed below.

| Jar Size | Process Time | Dial Gauge Canner | Weighted Gauge Canner |
|---|---|---|---|
| Pints | 75 minutes | 11 lbs | 10 lbs |
| Quarts | 90 minutes | 11 lbs | 10 lbs |

*Notes: For a little extra flavor, you can add a pinch of dried herbs like oregano or thyme to each jar before processing.*

### RECIPE: CANNED VENISON

In our community, the menfolk go out hunting every fall, and we are blessed with an abundance of venison. It's a lean, flavorful meat that is wonderful when canned. The canning process tenderizes the meat, making it perfect for stews, pot pies, or simply served over noodles. This is a taste of autumn in a jar.

**Ingredients:**

- Venison, trimmed of all fat and silver skin, cut into 1-inch cubes
- Canning salt

**Instructions:**

1. You can either raw pack or hot pack the venison. For a raw pack, simply pack the raw meat cubes into hot jars, leaving 1-inch headspace.
2. For a hot pack, brown the venison cubes in a little oil in a skillet. Then pack the hot meat into hot jars, leaving 1-inch headspace.
3. Add 1 teaspoon of canning salt to each quart jar or ½ teaspoon to each pint jar.
4. Cover the meat with boiling water, broth, or tomato juice, leaving 1-inch headspace.
5. Remove air bubbles, wipe the jar rims, and adjust the two-piece caps.

6. Process in a pressure canner according to the times listed below.

| Jar Size | Process Time | Dial Gauge Canner | Weighted Gauge Canner |
|---|---|---|---|
| Pints | 75 minutes | 11 lbs | 10 lbs |
| Quarts | 90 minutes | 11 lbs | 10 lbs |

*Notes: Venison can sometimes have a gamey flavor. To reduce this, you can soak the meat in a saltwater brine (1 tablespoon of salt per quart of water) for an hour before canning.*

## RECIPE: CANNED RABBIT

Rabbit is a lean, delicate meat that we've always enjoyed. It's a sustainable and easy-to-raise source of protein, and canning is a wonderful way to preserve it. Canned rabbit is delicious in casseroles, salads, or simply shredded and served on a sandwich.

**Ingredients:**

- Rabbit, cleaned and cut into pieces
- Canning salt

**Instructions:**

1. You can either raw pack or hot pack the rabbit. For a raw pack, pack the raw rabbit pieces into hot jars, leaving 1-inch headspace.
2. For a hot pack, brown the rabbit pieces in a little oil in a skillet. Then pack the hot rabbit into hot jars, leaving 1-inch headspace.
3. Add 1 teaspoon of canning salt to each quart jar or ½ teaspoon to each pint jar.
4. Cover the meat with boiling water or broth, leaving 1-inch headspace.
5. Remove air bubbles, wipe the jar rims, and adjust the two-piece caps.
6. Process in a pressure canner according to the times listed below.

| Jar Size | Process Time | Dial Gauge Canner | Weighted Gauge Canner |
|---|---|---|---|
| Pints | 75 minutes | 11 lbs | 10 lbs |
| Quarts | 90 minutes | 11 lbs | 10 lbs |

*Notes: You can can the rabbit with the bones in or out. If you leave the bones in, it will make a richer broth.*

## RECIPE: CANNED FISH

If you are blessed to live near a lake or river, canning fish is a wonderful way to preserve your catch. Smoked fish can also be canned for a delicious, shelf-stable treat. Canned fish is perfect for making fish cakes, salads, or simply eating straight from the jar.

**Ingredients:**

- Fresh fish, cleaned and scaled
- Canning salt
- Vinegar or lemon juice (optional)

**Instructions:**

1. Remove the head, tail, and fins from the fish. You can leave the bones in or take them out. Cut the fish into jar-sized pieces.
2. Pack the fish tightly into hot pint jars, leaving 1-inch headspace.
3. Add ½ teaspoon of canning salt to each pint jar.
4. If you like, you can add 1 tablespoon of vinegar or lemon juice to each jar to help firm up the fish and dissolve the small bones.
5. Do not add any liquid. The fish will make its own juice.
6. Wipe the jar rims and adjust the two-piece caps.
7. Process in a pressure canner for 100 minutes at 11 lbs for a dial gauge canner or 10 lbs for a weighted gauge canner.

*Notes: This recipe is for pint jars only. It is not recommended to can fish in quart jars.*

## RECIPE: HEARTY CHILI CON CARNE

There's nothing better on a cold winter's day than a bowl of hot chili. This is a complete meal in a jar, ready to heat and eat. I like to serve it with a dollop of sour cream and a sprinkle of sharp cheddar cheese. It's a comforting and satisfying meal that will warm you from the inside out.

**Ingredients:**

- 2 pounds ground beef
- 1 cup chopped onion
- 1 cup chopped green pepper
- 2 cloves garlic, minced
- 4 cups cooked kidney beans
- 4 cups tomato sauce
- 2 tablespoons chili powder
- 1 teaspoon cumin
- 1 teaspoon salt
- ½ teaspoon black pepper

**Instructions:**

1. Brown the ground beef, onion, and green pepper in a large skillet. Drain off the fat.
2. Add the garlic, kidney beans, tomato sauce, and spices. Simmer for 10 minutes.
3. Pack the hot chili into hot pint or quart jars, leaving 1-inch headspace.
4. Remove air bubbles, wipe the jar rims, and adjust the two-piece caps.
5. Process in a pressure canner according to the times listed below.

| Jar Size | Process Time | Dial Gauge Canner | Weighted Gauge Canner |
|----------|-------------|-------------------|-----------------------|
| Pints | 75 minutes | 11 lbs | 10 lbs |
| Quarts | 90 minutes | 11 lbs | 10 lbs |

*Notes: You can adjust the spiciness of the chili by adding more or less chili powder. For a thicker chili, you can add a can of tomato paste.*

## RECIPE: PANCETTA

Pancetta is an Italian-style bacon that is cured but not smoked. It's a versatile ingredient that can be used in a wide variety of dishes, from pasta sauces to salads. This is a simple recipe for a rolled pancetta that is easy to make and will add a touch of Italian flavor to your cooking.

### Ingredients:

- 5-pound slab of pork belly, skin off
- ¼ cup kosher salt
- 2 teaspoons pink salt #1
- 2 tablespoons brown sugar
- 2 tablespoons coarse-ground black pepper
- 1 tablespoon juniper berries, crushed
- 4 cloves garlic, minced

### Instructions:

1. Mix together all the ingredients except the pork belly.
2. Rub the mixture all over the pork belly.
3. Place the pork belly in a large, food-grade plastic bag and seal it, pressing out as much air as possible.
4. Refrigerate for 7 days, flipping the bag over every day.
5. After 7 days, remove the pork belly from the bag and rinse it well.
6. Pat the pork belly dry and roll it up tightly, fat side out. Tie it securely with butcher's twine.
7. Hang the pancetta in a cool, dry, well-ventilated place for 2-3 weeks, or until it has lost about 30% of its weight.

*Notes: You can also add other spices to your cure, like fennel seeds or red pepper flakes.*

## RECIPE: GUANCIALE

Guanciale is a rich, flavorful cured meat made from pork jowl. It's a key ingredient in many classic Italian dishes, like pasta carbonara and amatriciana. It's a simple cure, but the results are truly special. The fat in the jowl melts in your mouth, and the flavor is intensely porky and delicious.

**Ingredients:**

- 1 whole pork jowl, about 2-3 pounds
- ¼ cup kosher salt
- 2 teaspoons pink salt #1
- 2 tablespoons coarse-ground black pepper
- 1 tablespoon dried thyme

**Instructions:**

1. Trim any glands or ragged edges from the pork jowl.
2. Mix together the salt, pink salt #1, pepper, and thyme.
3. Rub the mixture all over the pork jowl.
4. Place the jowl in a food-grade plastic bag and seal it.
5. Refrigerate for 5-7 days, flipping the bag every day.
6. After 5-7 days, rinse the jowl well and pat it dry.
7. Poke a hole in one corner of the jowl and hang it in a cool, dry, well-ventilated place for at least 3 weeks, or until it is firm and has lost about 30% of its weight.

*Notes: Guanciale is best when it is aged for a longer period of time, up to 3 months.*

## RECIPE: LARDO

Lardo is a traditional Italian cured meat made from pork fatback. It's a delicacy that is prized for its rich, buttery texture and delicate flavor. It's wonderful sliced thin and served on warm bread, or used to flavor other dishes. This is a simple recipe that will introduce you to the magic of cured fat.

**Ingredients:**

- 2 pounds of pork fatback, skin on
- 1 cup of kosher salt
- 2 tablespoons of black pepper
- 1 tablespoon of fresh rosemary, chopped
- 4 cloves of garlic, minced

**Instructions:**

1. Mix together the salt, pepper, rosemary, and garlic.
2. Rub the mixture all over the fatback, making sure to cover all surfaces.

3. Place the fatback in a glass or ceramic container and cover it with the remaining salt mixture.
4. Cover the container and store it in a cool, dark place (like a root cellar or a cool basement) for at least 6 months.
5. After 6 months, the lardo will be firm and fragrant. To use it, simply scrape off the salt and slice it thin.

*Notes: The quality of your lardo will depend on the quality of your pork. Try to find the best quality pork fatback you can.*

## RECIPE: BRESAOLA

Bresaola is an Italian air-dried, salted beef that is lean and tender. It's a wonderful addition to a charcuterie board, or it can be sliced thin and served with a drizzle of olive oil and a squeeze of lemon juice. This is a simple recipe that will give you a taste of the Italian Alps.

**Ingredients:**

- 3-4 pound beef eye of round roast
- 1 cup of kosher salt
- ½ cup of brown sugar
- 2 tablespoons of black pepper
- 1 tablespoon of juniper berries, crushed
- 1 tablespoon of fresh rosemary, chopped

**Instructions:**

1. Trim all the fat and silver skin from the beef roast.
2. Mix together all the other ingredients.
3. Rub the mixture all over the beef roast.
4. Place the roast in a food-grade plastic bag and seal it.
5. Refrigerate for 10-14 days, flipping the bag every day.
6. After 10-14 days, rinse the roast well and pat it dry.
7. Wrap the roast in cheesecloth and hang it in a cool, dry, well-ventilated place for 3-4 weeks, or until it has lost about 30% of its weight.

*Notes: The ideal temperature for drying is around 50-60°F with a humidity of 60-70%.*

## RECIPE: TASSO HAM

Tasso ham is a spicy, smoky cured meat that is a specialty of Louisiana cuisine. It's not a ham in the traditional sense, but rather a cured and smoked pork shoulder. It's a key ingredient in many Cajun dishes, like jambalaya and gumbo. This is a simple recipe that will bring a taste of the bayou to your kitchen.

**Ingredients:**

- 4-5 pound pork shoulder, cut into 1-inch thick slices

- ½ cup of kosher salt
- ¼ cup of brown sugar
- 2 tablespoons of paprika
- 2 tablespoons of cayenne pepper
- 2 tablespoons of black pepper
- 1 tablespoon of white pepper
- 1 tablespoon of garlic powder
- 1 tablespoon of onion powder
- 2 teaspoons of pink salt #1

**Instructions:**

1. Mix together all the ingredients except the pork.
2. Rub the mixture all over the pork slices.
3. Place the pork in a food-grade plastic bag and seal it.
4. Refrigerate for 5-7 days, flipping the bag every day.
5. After 5-7 days, rinse the pork well and pat it dry.
6. Hot smoke the pork at 200-225°F for 2-3 hours, or until the internal temperature reaches 150°F (see Chapter 4 for more on smoking).

*Notes: Tasso ham is meant to be a flavoring ingredient, so it is very salty and spicy. A little goes a long way.*

# CHAPTER 2: PRESSURE CANNING – THE MODERN WORKHORSE OF AMISH PRESERVATION

I can still hear the soft rattle and hiss of the pressure canner on my mother's stove. The rhythmic sound of steam escaping through the weighted gauge was a comforting reminder that food was being put up for the winter — food that would nourish us when the snow lay thick and the roads were impassable. To this day, that sound means security to me. It means self-reliance.

In our Amish community, pressure canning was considered a modern marvel — a blessing that allowed us to safely preserve meats, soups, and full meals in jars without the need for ice or electricity. My mother used to say, *"A full row of jars on the pantry shelf is better than money in the bank."* And she was right.

Pressure canning is one of the most dependable ways to preserve meat safely and efficiently. It's the bridge between old-fashioned ways and modern convenience — and when done right, it can keep your family fed for years.

## UNDERSTANDING PRESSURE CANNING

Pressure canning works by heating food to **240°F or higher**, a temperature that can only be achieved under pressure. This heat destroys bacteria, including the spores that cause botulism — something a water bath canner can never do with low-acid foods like meat.

If you've never used a pressure canner before, don't be intimidated. It's a simple tool once you understand it. Think of it as an oven for jars. The canner does the work; you just prepare the ingredients and follow the correct times and pressures.

## THE BASICS: TIME, TEMPERATURE & PRESSURE

- **Dial Gauge Canners**: Process at 11 pounds pressure (adjust for altitude if above 2,000 feet).
- **Weighted Gauge Canners**: Process at 10 pounds pressure (15 lbs above 1,000 feet).
- **Processing Time**: 75 minutes for pints, 90 minutes for quarts (unless otherwise noted).

Always ensure:

1. Jars are hot and clean.
2. Lids are new and bands are in good condition.
3. Air bubbles are removed before sealing.
4. The canner cools naturally — never force it open.

### Equipment You'll Need

- A pressure canner (not pressure cooker)
- Standard mason jars and lids
- Jar lifter, funnel, ladle
- Towels and vinegar (for wiping rims)
- Patience — rushing is the enemy of good canning

### Recipes

Below are time-tested Amish-style pressure canning recipes — hearty, practical, and shelf-stable for up to 1–2 years.

## CANNED CHICKEN BREASTS

There's nothing handier than jars of tender chicken ready for soups, casseroles, or sandwiches.

### Ingredients:
• Boneless chicken breasts, cut into chunks
• Canning salt

### Instructions:

1. Pack raw chicken pieces into hot jars, leaving 1-inch headspace.
2. Add ½ tsp canning salt per pint, 1 tsp per quart.
3. Do **not** add liquid — the meat will create its own broth.
4. Wipe rims, apply lids, and process 75 min (pints) or 90 min (quarts).

*Notes: Great for chicken salad or pot pie.*

## CANNED BEEF STEW

A full meal in a jar — perfect for busy winter nights.

**Ingredients:**
- 2 lbs stewing beef
- 2 cups diced potatoes
- 1 cup carrots
- 1 cup onion
- 2 tsp salt, ½ tsp pepper
- 4 cups beef broth

**Instructions:**

1. Brown beef lightly in skillet.
2. Combine all ingredients; simmer 10 minutes.
3. Pack hot mixture into hot jars, leaving 1-inch headspace.
4. Process 75 min (pints) or 90 min (quarts).

*Notes: Add peas or corn after opening, not before canning.*

## PORK IN GRAVY

Tender pork cubes in a rich brown gravy — excellent over mashed potatoes.

**Ingredients:**
- 3 lbs pork shoulder, cubed
- ¼ cup flour
- Salt and pepper to taste
- 1 quart broth

**Instructions:**

1. Brown pork in batches, dusted lightly in flour.
2. Add broth, simmer until thickened slightly.
3. Pack into jars with 1-inch headspace.
4. Process 75 min (pints), 90 min (quarts).

**Notes:** A great way to use tougher cuts of pork.

## CANNED MEATBALLS IN TOMATO SAUCE

Perfect for spaghetti night or subs in minutes.

**Ingredients:**
- 2 lbs ground beef
- ½ cup breadcrumbs
- 1 egg
- 1 qt tomato sauce
- 1 tsp salt, ½ tsp oregano

**Instructions:**

1. Mix beef, breadcrumbs, egg, salt; form meatballs.
2. Brown lightly, then pack into jars.
3. Pour hot tomato sauce over, leaving 1-inch headspace.
4. Process 75 min (pints), 90 min (quarts).

**Notes:** Avoid dairy fillers in canned meatballs — they affect shelf life.

## CANNED BEEF ROAST

Juicy, tender roast that falls apart with a fork.

**Ingredients:**
• 3–4 lbs beef roast, cubed or sliced
• Salt and pepper
• Boiling water or broth

**Instructions:**

1. Pack raw meat into jars, leaving 1-inch headspace.
2. Add salt (1 tsp/quart).
3. Cover with boiling broth.
4. Process 75 min (pints), 90 min (quarts).

*Notes: Perfect base for beef and noodles.*

## CANNED HAM & BEAN SOUP

A true Amish favorite — hearty and humble.

**Ingredients:**
• 2 cups cooked navy beans
• 1 cup diced ham
• 1 cup onion
• 1 cup carrots
• 1 tsp salt, ½ tsp pepper
• 6 cups broth

**Instructions:**

1. Mix all ingredients; bring to a simmer.
2. Pack into jars, leaving 1-inch headspace.
3. Process 75 min (pints), 90 min (quarts).

*Notes: Beans should be pre-soaked and partially cooked.*

## SPICED CANNED SAUSAGE PATTIES

These patties keep beautifully and fry up like fresh.

**Ingredients:**
- 3 lbs ground pork
- 1 tbsp salt
- 1 tsp sage
- ½ tsp pepper
- ¼ tsp nutmeg

**Instructions:**
1. Mix spices into pork; form patties.
2. Brown lightly, pack into jars.
3. Pour boiling broth over, leaving 1-inch headspace.
4. Process 75 min (pints), 90 min (quarts).

*Notes: Drain fat well to ensure a clean seal.*

### CANNED TURKEY IN BROTH

A holiday lifesaver — shelf-stable leftover turkey.

**Ingredients:**
- Cooked turkey meat, cubed
- Boiling broth or water
- Salt (½ tsp/pint, 1 tsp/quart)

**Instructions:**
1. Pack hot jars with turkey, add boiling broth.
2. Remove bubbles, leaving 1-inch headspace.
3. Process 75 min (pints), 90 min (quarts).

*Notes: Great for quick turkey noodle soup.*

### CANNED BEEF STROGANOFF BASE

Creamy-style beef that can be finished with sour cream when serving.

**Ingredients:**
- 2 lbs beef strips
- 1 onion, sliced
- 1 clove garlic, minced
- 1 tsp salt
- ½ tsp pepper
- 2 cups beef broth

**Instructions:**
1. Brown beef and onion lightly.
2. Add broth; simmer 10 minutes.

3. Pack hot into jars with 1-inch headspace.
4. Process 75 min (pints), 90 min (quarts).

*Notes: Add cream after opening, never before canning.*

## AMISH BEEF & VEGETABLE SOUP

Every family had their own version of this — hearty and colorful.

**Ingredients:**
- 1 lb ground beef, browned
- 1 cup diced potatoes
- 1 cup carrots
- 1 cup corn
- 1 cup tomatoes
- 1 tsp salt
- ½ tsp pepper

**Instructions:**

1. Combine all ingredients; simmer 10 minutes.
2. Pack hot into jars with 1-inch headspace.
3. Process 75 min (pints), 90 min (quarts).

*Notes: A perfect base soup to customize with herbs when served.*

## QUICK PRESSURE CANNING RECIPES – AMISH PANTRY FAVORITES

| Recipe Name | Main Ingredients | Instructions (Condensed) | Notes & Serving Ideas |
|---|---|---|---|
| Canned Roast Chicken with Herbs | Chicken pieces, broth, thyme, rosemary, canning salt | Pack raw chicken and herbs into hot jars, add boiling broth, leave 1" headspace. Process 75 min (pints), 90 min (quarts). | Perfect for casseroles, pot pies, or chicken salad. |
| Beef Tips in Onion Gravy | Cubed beef, onions, broth, flour, salt | Brown beef and onions; add broth thickened with a little flour. Pack hot; process 75/90 min. | Serve over noodles, rice, or mashed potatoes. |
| Venison & Potato Stew | Venison, diced potatoes, carrots, celery, broth | Brown meat lightly, mix with vegetables and broth. Pack hot, 1" headspace, process 75/90 min. | A hearty winter staple. |
| Amish Chicken & Dumplings Base | Chicken, carrots, celery, broth, salt | Combine and simmer briefly. Pack hot, process 75/90 min. | Add dumplings fresh when reheating. |
| Pork & Sauerkraut Dinner | Cubed pork, sauerkraut, apple slices, broth | Layer pork, apples, and sauerkraut. Add broth, process 75/90 min. | Traditional New Year's meal. |
| Beef Chili Base | Ground beef, tomatoes, beans, chili spice | Brown beef; mix with tomatoes and spices; pack hot; process 75/90 min. | Add corn or cheese when serving. |

| Recipe Name | Main Ingredients | Instructions (Condensed) | Notes & Serving Ideas |
|---|---|---|---|
| Turkey & Wild Rice Soup | Cooked turkey, wild rice, onion, carrots, broth | Mix cooked ingredients; pack hot; process 75/90 min. | Ideal for leftover holiday turkey. |
| Ham & Lentil Soup | Diced ham, lentils, carrots, onion, celery, broth | Combine and simmer 10 min. Pack and process 75/90 min. | Thickens naturally as it sits. |
| Sweet & Sour Pork | Pork cubes, vinegar, sugar, peppers, pineapple | Parboil pork; mix sauce; pack hot; process 75/90 min. | Serve over rice or noodles. |
| Italian Meat Sauce | Ground beef, tomato purée, onion, garlic, basil | Brown meat, simmer in sauce, pack hot, process 75/90 min. | Excellent spaghetti base. |
| Beef Barley Soup | Beef cubes, barley, carrots, celery, onion, broth | Combine all; simmer 10 min; pack and process. | Fills the pantry with aroma of Sunday supper. |
| Amish Sloppy Joe Mix | Ground beef, tomato paste, brown sugar, vinegar, mustard | Brown meat; simmer sauce; pack hot, process 75/90 min. | Reheat for quick sandwiches. |
| Rabbit in White Gravy | Rabbit pieces, broth, flour, pepper, salt | Brown lightly, thicken gravy, pack and process 75/90 min. | Delicious over biscuits or noodles. |
| Chicken Corn Chowder Base | Chicken, corn, potatoes, onion, broth | Combine all; pack hot; process 75/90 min. | Add cream or butter when serving. |
| Canned Meatloaf Patties | Beef patties, broth, salt | Brown lightly, stack in jars, add broth, process 75/90 min. | Great for sandwiches or gravies. |
| Sausage & Bean Soup | Smoked sausage, beans, tomato, onion, celery | Combine all; bring to simmer; pack and process. | Rich, smoky flavor that deepens with age. |
| Spiced Canned Meat Mix | Ground beef/pork blend, onions, garlic, pepper | Brown lightly, drain, pack and process. | Multipurpose meat for casseroles or tacos. |
| Corned Venison Hash | Venison, potatoes, onion, salt, pickling spice | Cook lightly, mix with brine, pack hot, process 75/90 min. | Great breakfast side with eggs. |
| Beef Mushroom Gravy | Cubed beef, mushrooms, broth, flour, pepper | Brown beef, add mushrooms and broth, thicken slightly. Process 75/90 min. | Serve over mashed potatoes or rice. |
| Turkey Pot Pie Filling | Cooked turkey, peas, carrots, potatoes, broth | Combine; pack hot; process 75/90 min. | Add crust topping or biscuits when reheating. |

*Processing Notes: All recipes are designed for **pressure canning only**. Process pints = 75 minutes; quarts = 90 minutes at **10 lbs pressure (weighted gauge)** or **11 lbs (dial gauge)**. Adjust for altitude above 1,000 feet. Always remove air bubbles, leave 1 inch headspace, and let canner cool naturally.*

# CHAPTER 3: SALT CURING & BRINING – PRESERVING WITH THE POWER OF SALT

When I was a girl, butchering day was one of the busiest times of the year. My father and brothers would bring home the hogs, and before long, every surface of the kitchen and smokehouse would be filled with fresh cuts of meat ready to be cured. The air was cold and smelled of fresh pork, brown sugar, and smoke from the wood stove.

My mother's hands never stopped moving. She measured salt with an instinct born of experience, rubbed it into the meat, and carefully packed each piece into a wooden barrel. "This is how we store summer's work for winter," she'd say with quiet pride.

Salt curing is one of the oldest and most reliable preservation methods known to man. Long before freezers and pressure canners, our ancestors learned that salt — simple, pure salt — could keep meat safe for months or even years. When combined with sugar, spices, and time, it transforms meat into something remarkable: flavorful, tender, and deeply satisfying.

## THE SCIENCE BEHIND SALT PRESERVATION

Salt works its magic by drawing moisture out of both the meat and any bacteria that might cause spoilage. Without moisture, bacteria can't grow. The result is a piece of meat that's stable, flavorful, and safe for long-term storage.

There are two main ways to preserve meat with salt: **dry curing** and **brining**.

- **Dry Curing** means rubbing the meat with salt, sugar, and spices and allowing it to cure under refrigeration or in a cool environment. This is used for hams, bacon, and country-style cuts.

- **Brining** involves soaking meat in a saltwater solution infused with spices or sweeteners. This method adds moisture and tenderness while preserving flavor — perfect for corned beef, poultry, and fish.

## THE ROLE OF SUGAR AND SPICES

Sugar doesn't just add sweetness — it helps balance the sharpness of salt and encourages a mild fermentation that enhances flavor. Spices like pepper, bay, cloves, and mustard seed add depth and individuality to each recipe.

Every Amish household had its own curing mix, guarded like a family secret. The same combination of ingredients could be used year after year, with only minor adjustments to suit the harvest or the season.

## USING CURING SALTS SAFELY

For meats cured over long periods or those intended for smoking or drying, use **Pink Salt #1** or **#2** as described in Appendix B. These salts contain nitrites and nitrates that prevent botulism and preserve the meat's rosy color. Use only in small, measured amounts — never more than what the recipe specifies.

## THE IDEAL CURING ENVIRONMENT

Curing works best in a **cool, humid space** — between 34°F and 50°F, with moderate airflow. Traditionally, a cellar or smokehouse worked perfectly. Modern homesteaders can use a dedicated refrigerator or curing chamber to maintain consistent conditions.

## COUNTRY HAM

The pride of every Amish smokehouse — sweet, salty, and full of character.

**Ingredients:**
- 1 whole fresh ham (15–20 lbs)
- 1 cup kosher salt
- ½ cup brown sugar
- 2 tbsp black pepper
- 1 tbsp pink salt #2

**Instructions:**
1. Mix salt, sugar, pepper, and pink salt.
2. Rub the mixture thoroughly into the ham.
3. Place the ham in a wooden box or tub, skin side down.

4. Cover with remaining salt mix. Store at 38–40°F for 2 days per pound.
5. Remove, rinse, and hang to dry for 2 weeks.
6. Optionally, smoke for 3–5 days before aging in a cool space for 2–3 months.

*Notes: The longer it ages, the deeper the flavor.*

## SWEET-CURED BACON

This is the bacon I grew up on — rich, smoky, and slightly sweet from brown sugar and maple syrup.

**Ingredients:**
• 5 lbs pork belly
• ¼ cup kosher salt
• 2 tbsp brown sugar
• 1 tbsp black pepper
• 2 tsp pink salt #1
• ¼ cup maple syrup

**Instructions:**
1. Rub mixture into pork belly on all sides.
2. Place in a large food-safe bag or pan.
3. Cure in refrigerator for 7 days, flipping daily.
4. Rinse, pat dry, and air-dry 12 hours.
5. Smoke or bake at 200°F until internal temperature reaches 150°F.

*Notes: Slice thin and store frozen or vacuum-sealed.*

## CORNED BEEF BRINE

A classic brine for brisket that keeps beautifully and makes tender, flavorful beef.

**Ingredients:**
• 1 gallon water
• 1 cup kosher salt
• ½ cup brown sugar
• 2 tsp pink salt #1
• 2 tbsp pickling spice
• 4 cloves garlic, smashed

**Instructions:**
1. Bring all ingredients to a boil, then cool completely.
2. Submerge a 5–6 lb brisket in the brine.
3. Refrigerate 5–7 days, turning daily.

4. Rinse before cooking or pressure canning.

*Notes: Perfect for corned beef and cabbage or Reuben sandwiches.*

## BRINED TURKEY

Tender, juicy turkey without refrigeration — just like Grandma made before Thanksgiving.

**Ingredients:**
- 1 whole turkey (12–14 lbs)
- 2 gallons water
- 1½ cups salt
- 1 cup brown sugar
- 1 tbsp peppercorns
- 1 tbsp mustard seeds
- 4 bay leaves

**Instructions:**
1. Dissolve salt and sugar in warm water. Add spices; cool.
2. Submerge turkey completely.
3. Brine 24 hours under refrigeration or in a cool space.
4. Rinse well and roast or smoke immediately.

*Notes: Also works beautifully for chicken or game birds.*

## SALTED FISH (OLD-STYLE LAKE PRESERVATION)

Perfect for anyone near rivers or lakes — this simple method predates canning entirely.

**Ingredients:**
- Fresh fish fillets
- Coarse salt

**Instructions:**
1. Layer fish and salt in a crock — ½ inch salt between layers.
2. Weight with a plate and store cool for 3–5 days.
3. Rinse well, then dry or smoke for long storage.

*Notes: For mild flavor, soak salted fish in milk before cooking.*

## SUGAR-CURED PORK LOIN

A mild, sweet cure excellent for slicing thin for sandwiches.

**Ingredients:**
- 4 lbs pork loin
- ½ cup kosher salt
- ¼ cup brown sugar
- 1 tbsp pink salt #1
- 1 tbsp black pepper

**Instructions:**
1. Combine all ingredients and rub over pork.
2. Seal in plastic bag or covered container.
3. Cure 7 days, flipping daily.
4. Rinse, dry, and bake at 200°F until 150°F internal temperature.

*Notes: Slice thin; keeps refrigerated for weeks or frozen for months.*

## HONEY-CURED HAM

For those who prefer a sweeter ham with a golden glaze and mild flavor.

**Ingredients:**
- 1 fresh ham (10–12 lbs)
- 1 cup salt
- ½ cup honey
- ¼ cup brown sugar
- 2 tsp pink salt #1

**Instructions:**
1. Warm honey to thin it. Mix with salt and sugar.
2. Rub mixture into ham.
3. Cure 7–10 days per inch of thickness.
4. Rinse, dry, and smoke if desired.

**Notes:** Honey adds a beautiful color and subtle aroma.

## PICKLED TONGUE

A beloved old-fashioned delicacy that makes tender, flavorful meat slices.

**Ingredients:**
- 1 beef tongue
- 1 gallon water
- 1 cup salt
- ½ cup sugar
- 2 tsp pink salt #1
- 2 bay leaves, 10 peppercorns

**Instructions:**

1. Combine all ingredients; simmer and cool to room temperature.
2. Submerge tongue and cure for 10 days, turning daily.
3. Rinse well and simmer until tender. Peel skin before serving.

*Notes: Slice thin; serve cold with mustard.*

## AMISH PICKLED PORK

A country classic — pork cubes soaked in a vinegar-salt brine for quick preservation.

**Ingredients:**
- 3 lbs pork shoulder, cut in cubes
- 1 quart water
- 1 cup apple cider vinegar
- ½ cup salt
- 2 tbsp sugar
- 1 tbsp pickling spice

**Instructions:**

1. Combine brine ingredients and bring to a boil.
2. Add pork cubes; simmer 15 minutes.
3. Pack hot meat into jars, pour hot brine over.
4. Seal and refrigerate up to 3 months.

**Notes:** Great fried or served cold.

## SALT-CURED BEEF JERKY STRIPS

A shelf-stable, portable protein made the old way — with nothing but salt, time, and patience.

**Ingredients:**
- 2 lbs lean beef
- ½ cup salt
- 2 tbsp brown sugar
- 1 tbsp black pepper

**Instructions:**

1. Slice beef thin. Rub thoroughly with mixture.
2. Layer in crock and cover tightly.
3. Cure 5–7 days, then rinse.
4. Hang to air dry or smoke lightly.

*Notes: Properly cured and dried, jerky will last for months in a cool place.*

## QUICK SALT CURING & BRINING RECIPES – AMISH SMOKEHOUSE FAVORITES

| Recipe Name | Main Ingredients | Instructions (Condensed) | Notes & Serving Ideas |
|---|---|---|---|
| Simple Country Ham | Fresh ham, kosher salt, brown sugar, pink salt #2 | Rub mix on all sides; cure 2 days per lb at 38°F. Rinse, hang to dry, optional smoke. | Classic Amish ham, keeps 6+ months. |
| Brown Sugar Bacon | Pork belly, salt, brown sugar, pink salt #1, black pepper | Rub mixture on belly, cure 7 days turning daily, rinse, air-dry 12 hrs, smoke to 150°F. | Sweet, smoky, and beautifully marbled. |
| Honey-Cured Ham Slices | Ham slices, salt, honey, pink salt #1 | Mix cure; rub slices and layer in crock. Cure 5–7 days cold, rinse, dry, cook or smoke. | Mild, sweet flavor with golden color. |
| Corned Beef Brisket | Brisket, water, salt, brown sugar, pickling spice, pink salt #1 | Dissolve ingredients, cool, brine 5–7 days turning daily. Rinse before cooking. | Perfect for boiled dinners or sandwiches. |
| Pickled Pork Chops | Pork chops, vinegar, water, salt, sugar, bay leaves, peppercorns | Boil brine, cool, pour over chops. Cure 3–5 days refrigerated. | Fry or grill; tangy and tender. |
| Molasses-Cured Ham Ends | Ham ends, salt, molasses, black pepper | Rub thoroughly, cure 5–7 days, rinse and air dry. | Great for bean soups or seasoning meat. |
| Salt Brine for Poultry | Whole chickens, water, salt, brown sugar, bay leaves | Dissolve salt/sugar in warm water; cool; soak chicken 12–24 hrs. Rinse and roast or smoke. | Moist, flavorful meat every time. |
| Spiced Pickled Tongue | Beef tongue, water, salt, sugar, vinegar, bay, peppercorns | Boil brine, cool, pour over tongue, cure 10 days. Rinse, simmer till tender. | Slice thin for sandwiches. |
| Salt-Cured Fish Fillets | Fresh fish, coarse salt | Layer fish and salt in crock, cure 3–5 days cold. Rinse and air dry or smoke. | Traditional method for long storage. |
| Sugar-Cured Pork Loin | Pork loin, salt, brown sugar, pink salt #1, black pepper | Rub mixture over meat, cure 7 days refrigerated, rinse, bake or smoke. | Slice thin; great for sandwiches. |

## Processing & Storage Notes

- **Dry Cures:** Keep between 34–50°F with moderate humidity.
- **Brines:** Use non-reactive containers (glass, enamel, or food-safe plastic).
- **Storage:** Once cured, rinse and hang or refrigerate wrapped in cloth. Shelf-life varies from 2–6 months depending on conditions.

# CHAPTER 4: SMOKING - FLAVOR AND PRESERVATION COMBINED

There's a certain smell that takes me right back to my childhood: the sweet, fragrant aroma of applewood smoke drifting from our smokehouse on a crisp autumn afternoon. My father, a man of few words but great skill, would be tending the fire, his weathered hands carefully adding logs to keep the smoke just right. Inside the smokehouse, rows of sausages, hams, and fish would be slowly turning a beautiful, deep mahogany color, absorbing the flavor of the smoke and the wisdom of generations.

Smoking is a magical process. It's where preservation and flavor come together in a perfect marriage. The smoke not only adds a delicious, complex taste to the meat but also acts as a natural preservative, helping to protect it from spoilage. It's a technique that has been used for thousands of years, and for good reason: it works.

In this chapter, we'll explore the art of smoking, from the difference between cold smoking and hot smoking to how to build your own simple smokehouse. I'll also share with you some of my favorite recipes for smoked meats, the ones that have graced our family's table for as long as I can remember.

## COLD SMOKE VS. HOT SMOKE: THE CRITICAL DIFFERENCE

When we talk about smoking, we're really talking about two different methods: cold smoking and hot smoking. It's important to understand the difference, because they are used for different purposes.

- **Cold Smoking**: This is the true preservation method. In cold smoking, the temperature in the smokehouse is kept below 85°F. The meat is slowly smoked for hours, or even days, allowing the smoke to penetrate deeply and cure the meat without cooking it. Cold-smoked meats, like salami and some types of bacon, are then air-dried and can be stored for long periods.

- **Hot Smoking**: This method is more about flavor than preservation. In hot smoking, the temperature is high enough to cook the meat, typically between 200°F and 250°F. Hot-smoked meats, like barbecue ribs and smoked turkey, are fully cooked and have a wonderful smoky flavor, but they are not preserved and must be eaten right away or refrigerated.

In this chapter, we'll focus mainly on hot smoking, as it's the most accessible method for the home cook. But we'll also touch on cold smoking and how you can adapt some of the recipes.

## THE INVISIBLE SMOKE COMPOUNDS THAT PREVENT RANCIDITY

Have you ever wondered why smoked meats last so much longer than fresh meats? It's not just because of the drying effect of the smoke. The smoke itself contains hundreds of natural chemical compounds, some of which are powerful preservatives. These compounds, like phenols and aldehydes, have antimicrobial properties that inhibit the growth of bacteria. They also have antioxidant properties that prevent the fats in the meat from going rancid, which is one of the main causes of spoilage.

## HOW TO BUILD A SIMPLE SMOKEHOUSE FROM SCRAP MATERIALS

You don't need a fancy, expensive smoker to make delicious smoked meats at home. In fact, my father's smokehouse was built from salvaged barn wood and a few pieces of tin roofing. All you really need is a small, enclosed space to hold the smoke and a way to generate smoke from a fire.

A simple smokehouse can be built from a wooden box, an old refrigerator, or even a cardboard box. The key is to have a place for the fire to be separate from the food, with a pipe or a trench to carry the smoke to the smokehouse. This is especially important for cold smoking, where you need to keep the temperature low.

For hot smoking, you can use a charcoal or gas grill with a lid. Simply place your wood chips in a foil packet or a smoker box and place them on the hot coals or over the burner. The meat is then placed on the grill rack, away from the direct heat, and the lid is closed to trap the smoke.

## SELECTING THE RIGHT WOOD

The type of wood you use for smoking will have a big impact on the flavor of your meat. Different woods have different flavor profiles, and it's fun to experiment to see which ones you like best. Here are a few of my favorites:

- **Hickory**: This is the classic smoking wood, with a strong, bacon-like flavor. It's great for pork and beef.

- **Apple**: This is a mild, sweet wood that is wonderful with poultry and pork.

• **Mesquite**: This is a strong, earthy wood that is popular in Texas-style barbecue. It's best for beef and other dark meats.

• **Alder**: This is a delicate wood with a slightly sweet flavor. It's the traditional wood for smoking salmon.

Now, let's get to the recipes. We'll start with a simple smoked sausage that is a favorite in our family.

## RECIPE: SMOKED SAUSAGE

There's nothing quite like the taste of homemade smoked sausage. It's a world away from the bland, mass-produced sausages you find at the supermarket. This is a simple recipe that you can adapt to your own tastes. I like to make a big batch of this in the fall and hang it in the smokehouse to cure. It's a taste of home that I know you'll love.

**Ingredients:**

- 5 pounds of ground pork
- 1/4 cup of kosher salt
- 2 teaspoons of pink salt #1
- 2 tablespoons of brown sugar
- 2 tablespoons of paprika
- 1 tablespoon of black pepper
- 1 tablespoon of sage
- 1 teaspoon of cayenne pepper
- 1 cup of ice water
- Hog casings

**Instructions:**

1. In a large bowl, mix together all the ingredients except the water and casings. Mix well to distribute the spices evenly.
2. Add the ice water and mix until the sausage is sticky.
3. Stuff the sausage into the hog casings, twisting into 6-inch links.
4. Hang the sausages in a cool, dry place to dry for a few hours, until a pellicle forms.
5. Hot smoke the sausages at 200-225°F for 2-3 hours, or until the internal temperature reaches 150°F.

*Notes: You can also cold smoke these sausages for a more traditional cured sausage. Cold smoke at below 85°F for 6-8 hours.*

## RECIPE: SMOKED FISH

If you're lucky enough to have a fisherman in the family, this is a wonderful way to preserve the catch. Smoked fish is a delicacy that is prized for its rich, smoky flavor and firm, flaky texture. It's wonderful on its own, or you can use it to make a delicious smoked fish dip.

**Ingredients:**

- 5 pounds of fish fillets, such as salmon, trout, or mackerel
- 1 gallon of water
- 1 cup of kosher salt
- 1/2 cup of brown sugar

**Instructions:**

1. In a large container, mix together the water, salt, and sugar to make a brine. Stir until the salt and sugar are dissolved.
2. Place the fish fillets in the brine, making sure they are completely submerged.
3. Refrigerate for 4-6 hours.
4. Remove the fish from the brine and rinse it well under cold water.
5. Pat the fish dry and place it on a rack in a cool, dry place to form a pellicle.
6. Hot smoke the fish at 175-200°F for 2-3 hours, or until the fish is cooked through and flaky.

*Notes: For a sweeter smoked fish, you can brush it with maple syrup during the last hour of smoking.*

## RECIPE: SMOKED TURKEY

A smoked turkey is a beautiful and delicious centerpiece for any holiday meal. The smoke gives the turkey a wonderful flavor and a beautiful mahogany color. This is a simple recipe that will have your family and friends raving.

**Ingredients:**

- 1 whole turkey, 12-14 pounds
- 1 cup of kosher salt
- 1/2 cup of brown sugar
- 1 gallon of water
- 1 orange, quartered
- 1 onion, quartered
- 4 cloves of garlic, smashed
- 1 tablespoon of black peppercorns

**Instructions:**

1. In a large pot, combine the water, salt, and sugar. Bring to a boil, stirring to dissolve the salt and sugar. Remove from the heat and let it cool completely.
2. Add the orange, onion, garlic, and peppercorns to the cooled brine.
3. Place the turkey in a large, food-grade container and pour the brine over it. Make sure the turkey is completely submerged.
4. Refrigerate for 12-24 hours.
5. Remove the turkey from the brine and rinse it well, inside and out.

6.  Pat the turkey dry and place it on a rack in the refrigerator, uncovered, for at least 4 hours, or overnight.
7.  Hot smoke the turkey at 225-250°F for 6-8 hours, or until the internal temperature of the thigh reaches 165°F.

*Notes: You can stuff the cavity of the turkey with fresh herbs, like rosemary and thyme, for extra flavor.*

## RECIPE: SMOKED HAM

There's nothing quite like a homemade smoked ham. It's a labor of love, but it's well worth the effort. This is a traditional recipe for a cured and smoked ham that is perfect for a holiday feast or for slicing and serving on sandwiches.

**Ingredients:**

- 1 fresh ham, 15-20 pounds
- 1 cup of kosher salt
- 1/2 cup of brown sugar
- 2 tablespoons of pink salt #1
- 1/4 cup of black pepper
- 1/4 cup of paprika

**Instructions:**

1.  Mix together all the ingredients except the ham.
2.  Rub the mixture all over the ham, making sure to get it into all the nooks and crannies.
3.  Place the ham in a large, food-grade plastic bag and seal it.
4.  Refrigerate for 1 day per pound of ham, flipping the bag every day.
5.  After the curing time is up, remove the ham from the bag and rinse it well.
6.  Soak the ham in fresh water for 2-3 hours to remove some of the saltiness.
7.  Pat the ham dry and let it air dry for 24 hours.
8.  Hot smoke the ham at 225-250°F for 8-10 hours, or until the internal temperature reaches 150°F.

*Notes: You can glaze the ham with a mixture of brown sugar, mustard, and pineapple juice during the last hour of smoking.*

## RECIPE: SMOKED CHICKEN WINGS

Smoked chicken wings are a real treat. They're smoky, they're spicy, and they're incredibly addictive. This is a simple recipe that is perfect for a party or a game day get-together.

**Ingredients:**

- 5 pounds of chicken wings

- 1/4 cup of paprika
- 2 tablespoons of chili powder
- 2 tablespoons of brown sugar
- 1 tablespoon of black pepper
- 1 tablespoon of garlic powder
- 1 tablespoon of onion powder
- 1 teaspoon of cayenne pepper
- 2 tablespoons of salt

**Instructions:**

1. In a large bowl, mix together all the ingredients except the chicken wings.
2. Add the chicken wings and toss to coat.
3. Let the wings marinate for at least 4 hours, or overnight.
4. Hot smoke the wings at 250°F for 2-3 hours, or until they are cooked through and crispy.

*Notes: You can serve these wings with your favorite barbecue sauce or a creamy blue cheese dressing.*

## RECIPE: SMOKED PORK SHOULDER

Smoked pork shoulder, also known as pulled pork, is a classic barbecue dish that is loved by all. It's a simple cut of meat that is transformed into something truly special by the magic of smoke and time. This is a simple recipe that will give you tender, juicy pulled pork that is perfect for piling on a bun or serving with a side of coleslaw.

**Ingredients:**

- 1 pork shoulder, 6-8 pounds
- 1/4 cup of brown sugar
- 1/4 cup of paprika
- 2 tablespoons of black pepper
- 2 tablespoons of salt
- 1 tablespoon of garlic powder
- 1 tablespoon of onion powder
- 1 teaspoon of cayenne pepper

**Instructions:**

1. In a small bowl, mix together all the ingredients except the pork shoulder.
2. Rub the mixture all over the pork shoulder.
3. Wrap the pork shoulder in plastic wrap and refrigerate for at least 4 hours, or overnight.
4. Hot smoke the pork shoulder at 225-250°F for 10-12 hours, or until the internal temperature reaches 195°F.

5.  Let the pork shoulder rest for at least 30 minutes before shredding it with two forks.

*Notes: For extra moisture, you can place a pan of water in the smoker while the pork is cooking.*

## Recipe: Smoked Salmon

Smoked salmon is a true delicacy. It's a simple yet elegant dish that is perfect for a special occasion or a lazy Sunday brunch. This is a simple recipe for a hot-smoked salmon that is flaky, moist, and full of flavor.

**Ingredients:**

- 1 whole salmon fillet, about 3 pounds
- 1/4 cup of kosher salt
- 1/4 cup of brown sugar
- 1 tablespoon of black pepper

**Instructions:**

1.  In a small bowl, mix together the salt, sugar, and pepper.
2.  Rub the mixture all over the salmon fillet.
3.  Place the salmon in a glass dish, cover with plastic wrap, and refrigerate for 4-6 hours.
4.  Rinse the salmon well and pat it dry.
5.  Let the salmon air dry for 1-2 hours, until a pellicle forms.
6.  Hot smoke the salmon at 175-200°F for 1-2 hours, or until it is cooked through and flakes easily.

*Notes: You can serve the smoked salmon with cream cheese, capers, and red onion on a bagel.*

### RECIPE: SMOKED BEEF BRISKET

Smoked beef brisket is the king of Texas barbecue. It's a tough cut of meat that is transformed into something tender, juicy, and incredibly flavorful by the slow and low cooking process. This is a simple recipe that will give you a taste of the Lone Star State.

**Ingredients:**

- 1 whole beef brisket, 10-12 pounds
- 1/2 cup of kosher salt
- 1/2 cup of black pepper

**Instructions:**

1.  Trim the fat cap of the brisket to about 1/4 inch thick.

2. Mix together the salt and pepper.
3. Rub the mixture all over the brisket.
4. Let the brisket sit at room temperature for 1 hour.
5. Hot smoke the brisket at 250°F for 10-12 hours, or until the internal temperature reaches 200°F.
6. Let the brisket rest for at least 1 hour before slicing it against the grain.

*Notes: For a more complex flavor, you can add other spices to your rub, like garlic powder, onion powder, and chili powder.*

## RECIPE: SMOKED GOUDA CHEESE

Smoking is not just for meat. You can also smoke cheese, and the results are absolutely delicious. Smoked Gouda is a creamy, nutty cheese that is wonderful on its own or melted into a sandwich. This is a simple recipe that will introduce you to the world of smoked cheese.

**Ingredients:**

- 1 wheel of Gouda cheese, about 2 pounds

**Instructions:**

1. Cut the cheese into 1-inch thick slices.
2. Place the cheese on a rack in a cold smoker.
3. Cold smoke the cheese for 2-3 hours, keeping the temperature below 90°F.
4. Wrap the cheese in plastic wrap and refrigerate for at least 24 hours to let the smoke flavor mellow.

*Notes: You can also smoke other hard cheeses, like cheddar or provolone.*

## RECIPE: SMOKED ALMONDS

Smoked almonds are a delicious and healthy snack. They're a great addition to a charcuterie board, or you can just eat them by the handful. This is a simple recipe that will have you making your own smoked nuts all the time.

**Ingredients:**

- 2 cups of raw almonds
- 1 tablespoon of olive oil
- 1 teaspoon of salt
- 1/2 teaspoon of paprika

**Instructions:**

1. Preheat your smoker to 225°F.

2. In a bowl, toss the almonds with the olive oil, salt, and paprika.
3. Spread the almonds in a single layer on a baking sheet.
4. Smoke for 1-2 hours, or until the almonds are fragrant and lightly browned.

*Notes: You can also add other spices to your almonds, like chili powder or cumin.*

## QUICK SMOKING RECIPES – AMISH SMOKEHOUSE TRADITIONS

| Recipe Name | Main Ingredients | Instructions (Condensed) | Notes & Serving Ideas |
|---|---|---|---|
| Smoked Country Ham | Salt-cured ham, hickory or applewood chips | Hang cured ham in cool smoker, maintain 120–130°F for 3–5 days. | Deep smoky flavor; slice thin for sandwiches. |
| Hickory-Smoked Bacon | Cured pork belly, brown sugar, black pepper | After curing, smoke 6–8 hrs at 150°F until internal temp reaches 150°F. | Store cool or refrigerate; fry before serving. |
| Maple-Smoked Sausage Links | Ground pork, salt, brown sugar, sage, pink salt #1 | Stuff into casings, dry 1 hr, smoke at 160°F for 3 hrs. | Sweet, mild flavor perfect for breakfast. |
| Smoked Venison Jerky | Venison strips, salt, brown sugar, black pepper | Marinate 12 hrs, smoke at 140–160°F until dry but pliable. | High-protein trail snack. |
| Applewood-Smoked Chicken Quarters | Chicken quarters, salt brine, black pepper | Brine overnight, pat dry, smoke 3–4 hrs at 225°F. | Moist, flavorful meat for any meal. |
| Smoked Ham Hocks | Ham hocks, salt, molasses, bay leaf | Brine overnight, then smoke at 200°F for 4 hrs. | Use in soups or beans for rich flavor. |
| Smoked Turkey Breast | Turkey breast, salt brine, brown sugar | Brine 12 hrs, rinse, smoke at 225°F until 165°F internal. | Perfect centerpiece for Sunday dinner. |
| Smoked Beef Brisket | Brined brisket, black pepper, garlic powder | Smoke 8–10 hrs at 225°F until tender. Rest before slicing. | Classic Amish picnic meal. |
| Smoked Pork Chops | Salt-cured chops, brown sugar, pepper | Air-dry overnight, smoke 3–4 hrs at 180°F. | Delicious reheated or fried. |
| Smoked Trout Fillets | Trout fillets, salt brine, lemon, dill | Brine 2 hrs, rinse, pat dry, smoke at 160°F until firm. | Flaky and mild; pairs well with crackers or bread. |

# CHAPTER 5: DRYING & PEMMICAN - THE ULTIMATE SURVIVAL FOOD

I often think about my ancestors, the ones who crossed the great ocean to build a new life in this country. They came with very little, but they brought with them a wealth of knowledge, including the ancient art of drying meat. For them, drying meat wasn't a hobby; it was a matter of survival. It was a way to carry a lightweight, nutrient-dense food on long journeys and to have a source of protein during the lean winter months.

Of all the preservation methods, drying is the one that feels most elemental. It's the simple act of removing water, the one thing that all living things need to survive, including the bacteria that cause spoilage. It's a technique that has been used by cultures all over the world for thousands of years, and it's just as effective today as it was for our ancestors.

In this chapter, we're going to explore the world of dried meats, from traditional beef jerky to the ultimate survival food: pemmican. I'll show you how to turn a few pounds of fresh meat into a lightweight, shelf-stable food that can last for months, or even years, without refrigeration.

## THE DIFFERENCE BETWEEN JERKY AND PEMMICAN

People often use the terms "jerky" and "pemmican" interchangeably, but they are actually two very different things.

• Jerky is made from thin strips of meat that are marinated and then dried. It's a delicious, high-protein snack, but it still contains a small amount of moisture, which means it has a shorter shelf life than pemmican.

- Pemmican is a mixture of dried meat powder and rendered fat. It's not as tasty as jerky, but it's a true survival food. Because it contains almost no water, it can last for decades without spoiling. It's a compact, high-energy food that is perfect for a bug-out bag or a long-term food storage pantry.

## THE "BONE DRY" TEST FOR MEAT POWDER

When you're making pemmican, it's crucial that the meat be completely dry. Any moisture left in the meat can cause it to spoil. The way to test for this is what I call the "bone dry" test. After you've dried your meat, you should be able to grind it into a fine powder. If the meat is still flexible or chewy, it's not dry enough. It needs to be so dry that it shatters when you hit it with a hammer.

## HOW TO TURN 2.4 LBS OF MEAT INTO A PINT OF FOOD THAT NEVER SPOILS

It may seem hard to believe, but it's true. When you remove all the water from meat, you're left with a very concentrated source of protein. It takes about 2.4 pounds of fresh meat to make one pint of dried meat powder. When you mix that powder with rendered fat, you have a pint of pemmican, a food that is so shelf-stable it was once used to provision polar expeditions.

Now, let's get to the recipes. We'll start with a classic beef jerky that is a favorite in my family.

## RECIPE: TRADITIONAL BEEF JERKY

This is the jerky I grew up on. It's simple, it's savory, and it's the perfect snack for a long day of working in the fields. The secret to good jerky is to use a lean cut of meat and to slice it thin. The marinade is a simple one, but it gives the jerky a wonderful flavor.

**Ingredients:**

- 2 pounds of lean beef, such as eye of round or top round
- 1/2 cup of soy sauce
- 2 tablespoons of Worcestershire sauce
- 1 tablespoon of honey
- 1 teaspoon of black pepper
- 1 teaspoon of onion powder
- 1/2 teaspoon of garlic powder

**Instructions:**

1. Trim all the fat from the beef and slice it into thin strips, about 1/8 inch thick. It's easiest to do this if the meat is partially frozen.
2. In a bowl, mix together the soy sauce, Worcestershire sauce, honey, pepper, onion powder, and garlic powder.
3. Add the beef strips to the marinade and toss to coat.
4. Cover the bowl and refrigerate for at least 4 hours, or overnight.

5. Remove the beef from the marinade and pat it dry with paper towels.
6. Dry the jerky in a dehydrator at 145°F for 4-6 hours, or until it is dry and leathery.

*Notes: You can also dry the jerky in your oven on the lowest setting. Just prop the oven door open with a wooden spoon to allow the moisture to escape.*

## RECIPE: BASIC PEMMICAN

This is the real deal, the food that sustained the fur traders and explorers of old. It's not fancy, but it's a nutritional powerhouse. It's the perfect food for a long-term survival situation.

**Ingredients:**

- 1 pound of dried meat powder
- 1 pound of rendered beef tallow or lard
- Optional: 1/2 cup of dried berries, such as cranberries or blueberries

**Instructions:**

1. To make the dried meat powder, you'll need to dry lean meat until it is bone dry. Then, you can grind it into a powder using a blender, a coffee grinder, or a mortar and pestle.
2. In a large bowl, mix together the meat powder and the dried berries, if using.
3. Melt the tallow or lard in a saucepan over low heat.
4. Pour the melted fat over the meat powder and mix well.
5. Press the pemmican into a pan and let it cool completely.
6. Cut the pemmican into bars and wrap them in wax paper.

*Notes: Pemmican will last for years if stored in a cool, dark place.*

## RECIPE: TERIYAKI PORK JERKY

This is a sweet and savory jerky that is a favorite with the young folks in my family. It's a little bit of a modern twist on a classic, but it's so delicious that I just had to include it.

**Ingredients:**

- 2 pounds of lean pork, such as pork loin or tenderloin
- 1/2 cup of soy sauce
- 1/4 cup of brown sugar
- 2 tablespoons of rice vinegar
- 1 tablespoon of grated fresh ginger
- 2 cloves of garlic, minced

**Instructions:**

1. Slice the pork into thin strips, about 1/8 inch thick.
2. In a bowl, mix together the soy sauce, brown sugar, rice vinegar, ginger, and garlic.
3. Add the pork strips to the marinade and toss to coat.
4. Refrigerate for at least 4 hours, or overnight.
5. Dry the jerky in a dehydrator at 145°F for 4-6 hours, or until it is dry and leathery.

*Notes: For a little extra kick, you can add a pinch of red pepper flakes to the marinade.*

## RECIPE: VENISON JERKY

Venison makes a wonderful jerky. It's lean, it's flavorful, and it has a rich, earthy taste that is just delicious. This is a simple recipe that really lets the flavor of the venison shine through.

**Ingredients:**

- 2 pounds of venison, trimmed of all fat and silver skin
- 1/4 cup of soy sauce
- 2 tablespoons of Worcestershire sauce
- 1 tablespoon of black pepper
- 1 teaspoon of onion powder

**Instructions:**

1. Slice the venison into thin strips, about 1/8 inch thick.
2. In a bowl, mix together the soy sauce, Worcestershire sauce, pepper, and onion powder.
3. Add the venison strips to the marinade and toss to coat.
4. Refrigerate for at least 4 hours, or overnight.
5. Dry the jerky in a dehydrator at 145°F for 4-6 hours, or until it is dry and leathery.

*Notes: Venison can sometimes have a gamey flavor. To reduce this, you can soak the meat in a saltwater brine (1 tablespoon of salt per quart of water) for an hour before marinating.*

## RECIPE: TURKEY JERKY

Turkey jerky is a lean, healthy snack that is a great alternative to beef or pork jerky. It's a little milder in flavor, but it's still delicious. This is a simple recipe that is perfect for using up leftover turkey from a holiday meal.

**Ingredients:**

- 2 pounds of cooked turkey breast, sliced thin
- 1/4 cup of soy sauce
- 2 tablespoons of honey

- 1 tablespoon of lemon juice
- 1 teaspoon of smoked paprika

**Instructions:**

1. In a bowl, mix together the soy sauce, honey, lemon juice, and paprika.
2. Add the turkey slices to the marinade and toss to coat.
3. Refrigerate for at least 2 hours.
4. Dry the jerky in a dehydrator at 145°F for 3-5 hours, or until it is dry and leathery.

*Notes: You can also use raw turkey breast for this recipe. Just slice it thin and marinate it for at least 4 hours.*

## RECIPE: BILTONG

Biltong is a type of cured and dried meat that originated in Southern Africa. It's similar to jerky, but it's typically made with thicker cuts of meat and is cured with vinegar and spices before being air-dried. The result is a tender, flavorful dried meat that is a favorite in my family.

**Ingredients:**

- 2 pounds of beef, such as top round or sirloin, cut into 1-inch thick strips
- 1/4 cup of kosher salt
- 2 tablespoons of brown sugar
- 1 tablespoon of black pepper, coarsely ground
- 1 tablespoon of coriander, toasted and coarsely ground
- 1/2 cup of red wine vinegar

**Instructions:**

1. In a bowl, mix together the salt, sugar, pepper, and coriander.
2. Rub the mixture all over the beef strips.
3. Place the beef in a glass dish and pour the vinegar over it.
4. Cover and refrigerate for 24 hours, turning the meat once.
5. Remove the meat from the dish and pat it dry.
6. Hang the biltong in a cool, dry, well-ventilated place with a fan for 3-5 days, or until it is dry to your liking.

*Notes: You can also use a biltong box, which is a specially designed box with a fan and a light bulb to create the perfect drying environment.*

## RECIPE: SALMON JERKY

Salmon jerky is a delicious and healthy snack that is packed with omega-3 fatty acids. It's a great way to preserve a bountiful catch, and it's a favorite of the fishermen in my community. This is a simple recipe for a sweet and savory salmon jerky that is sure to please.

**Ingredients:**

- 2 pounds of salmon fillet, skin removed
- 1/2 cup of soy sauce
- 1/4 cup of maple syrup
- 1 tablespoon of brown sugar
- 1 teaspoon of black pepper

**Instructions:**

1. Slice the salmon into thin strips, about 1/4 inch thick.
2. In a bowl, mix together the soy sauce, maple syrup, brown sugar, and pepper.
3. Add the salmon strips to the marinade and toss to coat.
4. Refrigerate for 4-6 hours.
5. Dry the jerky in a dehydrator at 145°F for 4-6 hours, or until it is dry and firm.

*Notes: For a smoky flavor, you can add a teaspoon of liquid smoke to the marinade.*

### RECIPE: SPICY BEEF JERKY

For those who like a little heat, this spicy beef jerky is a real treat. It's got a kick to it, but it's not so hot that you can't taste the flavor of the beef. This is a favorite of my son, who always asks me to make a batch for him to take on his hunting trips.

**Ingredients:**

- 2 pounds of lean beef, such as eye of round or top round
- 1/2 cup of soy sauce
- 2 tablespoons of Worcestershire sauce
- 1 tablespoon of Sriracha or other hot sauce
- 1 tablespoon of brown sugar
- 1 teaspoon of red pepper flakes
- 1 teaspoon of black pepper

**Instructions:**

1. Slice the beef into thin strips, about 1/8 inch thick.
2. In a bowl, mix together all the other ingredients.
3. Add the beef strips to the marinade and toss to coat.
4. Refrigerate for at least 4 hours, or overnight.
5. Dry the jerky in a dehydrator at 145°F for 4-6 hours, or until it is dry and leathery.

*Notes: You can adjust the spiciness of this jerky by adding more or less hot sauce and red pepper flakes.*

## RECIPE: DROEWORS (DRIED SAUSAGE)

Droewors is a traditional South African dried sausage that is similar to biltong. It's made with a mixture of beef and pork and is seasoned with spices like coriander and nutmeg. It's a delicious and satisfying snack that is perfect for a long journey.

**Ingredients:**

- 1 pound of ground beef
- 1 pound of ground pork
- 2 tablespoons of kosher salt
- 1 tablespoon of black pepper, coarsely ground
- 1 tablespoon of coriander, toasted and coarsely ground
- 1 teaspoon of nutmeg
- 1/4 cup of red wine vinegar
- Hog casings

**Instructions:**

1. In a large bowl, mix together all the ingredients except the casings.
2. Stuff the mixture into the hog casings, creating one long rope of sausage.
3. Hang the sausage in a cool, dry, well-ventilated place with a fan for 3-5 days, or until it is dry and firm.

*Notes: You can also dry the droewors in a biltong box.*

## RECIPE: FRUIT PEMMICAN

This is a sweeter version of pemmican that is a favorite with the children in my community. The addition of dried fruit gives it a pleasant sweetness and a chewy texture. It's a great way to get a little extra energy on a long hike or a busy day.

**Ingredients:**

- 1 pound of dried meat powder
- 1 pound of rendered beef tallow or lard
- 1 cup of dried fruit, such as cranberries, cherries, or raisins
- Optional: 1/4 cup of honey or maple syrup

**Instructions:**

1. In a large bowl, mix together the meat powder and the dried fruit.
2. Melt the tallow or lard in a saucepan over low heat. If you're using honey or maple syrup, stir it into the melted fat.
3. Pour the melted fat over the meat and fruit mixture and mix well.
4. Press the pemmican into a pan and let it cool completely.
5. Cut the pemmican into bars and wrap them in wax paper.

*Notes: This pemmican will not last as long as the basic pemmican because of the moisture in the fruit, but it will still keep for several months in a cool, dark place.*

## QUICK DRYING & DEHYDRATION RECIPES – AMISH AIR-DRYING TRADITIONS

| Recipe Name | Main Ingredients | Instructions (Condensed) | Notes & Serving Ideas |
|---|---|---|---|
| Traditional Beef Jerky | Lean beef, salt, brown sugar, black pepper | Slice thin, marinate overnight, hang in warm, airy spot or dehydrate at 145°F until dry. | Classic trail snack; lasts months in a cool jar. |
| Venison Jerky with Molasses | Venison, molasses, salt, garlic, pepper | Marinate 12 hrs; dry in smoker or oven 150°F, 6–8 hrs. | Slightly sweet, smoky flavor. |
| Amish Smoked Sausage Chips | Cooked smoked sausage, pepper | Slice thin, dry at 150°F until crisp. | Great for soups or snacks. |
| Chicken Jerky Strips | Chicken breast, salt, honey, garlic powder | Slice thin, marinate, dehydrate at 145°F until leathery. | Mild and slightly sweet; rehydrates quickly. |
| Dried Ham Shavings | Ham slices, salt | Cut thin, dry on racks near stove until crisp. | Sprinkle in beans or eggs for flavor. |
| Beef & Onion Dry Soup Mix | Ground beef, dried onion, garlic, salt | Brown beef, drain, dry on tray 155°F until crumbly. Mix with onions. | Add boiling water for instant soup. |
| Turkey Jerky with Sage | Turkey breast, salt, sage, brown sugar | Slice thin, marinate, dry at 150°F until pliable. | Excellent high-protein snack. |
| Pork Crackle Bits | Rendered pork fat scraps, salt | Bake or air-dry until crisp. Store airtight. | Crunchy topping or snack. |
| Dried Soup Beef Base | Cubed beef, salt, pepper, onion | Simmer cubes briefly, dry on racks at 155°F until hard. | Drop into broths or stews. |
| Dried Chicken & Vegetable Mix | Cooked chicken, peas, carrots, celery | Dry all separately at 140°F, mix and store airtight. | Add to boiling water for quick soup. |

### Drying & Storage Notes

- **Temperature:** Keep between **140°F–160°F** for safe drying; lower for thinner slices.
- **Airflow:** Essential — use racks, not trays, to let air circulate.
- **Moisture Test:** Meat should bend and crack slightly, not snap.
- **Storage:** Store dried meats in airtight jars or vacuum-sealed pouches. Keep cool, dark, and dry. Shelf-life: **3–6 months**.

# CHAPTER 6: FAT PRESERVATION - POTTED MEAT & CONFIT

I remember my grandmother's cellar as a cool, dark wonderland, filled with the earthy smells of potatoes and onions, and the sweet scent of apples. But my favorite corner was where she kept the crocks of potted meat. Each crock was sealed with a thick layer of pure white lard, a protective blanket that kept the meat inside fresh and delicious for months on end. To me, it was magic. How could meat stay so good without being canned or frozen?

The answer, of course, is the magic of fat. Preserving meat in fat is one of the oldest and most delicious of all the preservation methods. It's a technique that has been largely forgotten in our modern world of refrigerators and freezers, but it's a skill that is well worth rediscovering. Not only is it a practical way to preserve meat without electricity, but it also produces some of the most tender, flavorful meat you will ever taste.

In this chapter, we're going to explore the lost art of fat preservation, from the simple potted meats of my grandmother's kitchen to the elegant confit of a French bistro. I'll show you how to render your own lard and tallow, how to properly cook and pack the meat, and how to create that all-important "fat seal" that will keep your meat safe and delicious for months to come.

## THE "FAT SEAL" METHOD FOR KEEPING MEAT FRESH FOR MONTHS

The principle behind fat preservation is simple: fat creates an airtight barrier that protects the meat from oxygen and bacteria. As long as the meat is completely submerged in fat and the container is sealed with a thick layer of fat, it will stay fresh and delicious for a very long time. This is the secret to my grandmother's potted meat, and it's the same principle that is used to make confit.

## WHY GRANDMA'S POTTED MEAT WAS SAFE (AND WHY MODERN KITCHENS ARE DIFFERENT)

Now, I know some of you may be a little hesitant about this method. We've all been taught to be wary of leaving meat out at room temperature. But the truth is, when it's done correctly, fat preservation is a very safe and effective method. The key is to make sure the meat is properly cooked and the container is properly sealed. In my grandmother's day, they didn't have to worry as much about the things we do today. Their kitchens were cooler, their meat was fresher, and they had a deep, intuitive understanding of these old ways. In our modern, centrally heated homes, we need to be a little more careful, but with a few simple precautions, you can safely and confidently preserve meat in fat.

## THE 1/4-INCH LARD LAYER THAT SEALS OUT BACTERIA

The most important part of fat preservation is the seal. After you've packed your meat into a crock or a jar, you need to cover it with a layer of melted lard or tallow that is at least 1/4 inch thick. As the fat cools, it will solidify and create an airtight seal that will protect the meat from spoilage. It's a simple but brilliant technique that has been used for centuries.

## RENDERING LARD/TALLOW

Before you can preserve meat in fat, you need to have a good supply of high-quality rendered lard or tallow. Rendering is the process of melting down animal fat to separate the pure fat from any bits of meat or connective tissue. It's a simple process that you can do at home, and it's a great way to use up the fat from a hog or a steer that might otherwise go to waste.

To render lard or tallow, simply chop the fat into small pieces and place it in a heavy-bottomed pot over low heat. As the fat melts, it will release the pure, liquid fat. Strain the liquid fat through a piece of cheesecloth to remove any solids, and then pour it into jars to cool. Once it's cooled, it will solidify into a creamy white fat that is perfect for preserving meat or for using in your cooking.

## THE CONFIT PROCESS

Confit is a French technique of slowly cooking meat in its own fat. It's a luxurious and delicious way to preserve meat, and it's surprisingly easy to do at home. The most famous confit is duck confit, but you can also make confit with chicken, pork, or even rabbit.

The process is simple: the meat is first cured in salt and spices, and then it is slowly cooked in a bath of melted fat until it is incredibly tender. The cooked meat is then packed into a crock or a jar and covered with the fat it was cooked in. The result is a meat that is so tender it practically melts in your mouth, with a rich, savory flavor that is simply divine.

## PACKING AND SEALING CROCKS

When you're preserving meat in fat, it's important to use the right kind of container. A ceramic crock is the traditional choice, but you can also use a glass jar. The most important thing is that the container is clean and dry.

Pack the cooked meat into the container, making sure to leave enough room at the top for the fat seal. Pour the melted fat over the meat, making sure it is completely submerged. Then, pour a final layer of fat on top that is at least 1/4 inch thick. Let the container cool completely, and then store it in a cool, dark place, like a root cellar or a cool basement.

Now, let's get to the recipes. We'll start with the classic duck confit.

## RECIPE: DUCK CONFIT

This is a dish that is fit for a king, but it's surprisingly simple to make at home. It's a taste of luxury that will transport you to a cozy French bistro. Serve it with some roasted potatoes and a simple green salad for a truly memorable meal.

**Ingredients:**

- 4 duck legs
- 1/4 cup of kosher salt
- 1 tablespoon of black pepper
- 4 cloves of garlic, smashed
- 4 sprigs of fresh thyme
- 4 cups of rendered duck fat, lard, or tallow

**Instructions:**

1. In a small bowl, mix together the salt and pepper.
2. Rub the mixture all over the duck legs.
3. Place the duck legs in a glass dish, top with the garlic and thyme, and cover with plastic wrap.
4. Refrigerate for 24 hours.
5. Preheat your oven to 225°F.
6. Rinse the duck legs well and pat them dry.
7. In a Dutch oven or a heavy-bottomed pot, melt the duck fat over low heat.
8. Submerge the duck legs in the melted fat.
9. Cook for 3-4 hours, or until the meat is very tender.
10. Let the duck legs cool in the fat.
11. To store, place the duck legs in a clean crock or jar and cover them with the fat. Make sure the fat seal is at least 1/4 inch thick.

*Notes: If you don't have enough duck fat, you can supplement it with lard or tallow.*

## RECIPE: PORK RILLETTES (POTTED PORK)

This is a rustic and delicious spread that is perfect for a picnic or a simple lunch. It's made from pork shoulder that is slowly cooked in its own fat until it is so tender it can be shredded with a fork. It's wonderful served on a piece of crusty bread with a sharp mustard and some cornichons.

**Ingredients:**

- 3 pounds of pork shoulder, cut into 1-inch cubes
- 1 pound of pork fatback, cut into 1-inch cubes
- 1 cup of water
- 1 tablespoon of salt
- 1 teaspoon of black pepper
- 2 cloves of garlic, smashed
- 2 sprigs of fresh thyme

**Instructions:**

1. In a heavy-bottomed pot, combine all the ingredients.
2. Bring to a simmer over low heat and cook for 3-4 hours, or until the pork is very tender.
3. Remove the pork from the pot and shred it with two forks.
4. Strain the fat from the pot and discard the solids.
5. Pack the shredded pork into a crock or a jar and pour the strained fat over it.
6. Let it cool completely and then store it in the refrigerator.

*Notes: Rillettes will keep in the refrigerator for several weeks.*

## RECIPE: CHICKEN CONFIT

This is a more economical version of duck confit, but it's just as delicious. It's a wonderful way to use up a whole chicken, and the result is a tender, flavorful meat that is perfect for a weeknight meal.

**Ingredients:**

- 1 whole chicken, cut into 8 pieces
- 1/4 cup of kosher salt
- 1 tablespoon of black pepper
- 4 cloves of garlic, smashed
- 4 sprigs of fresh thyme
- 4 cups of rendered chicken fat, lard, or tallow

**Instructions:**

1. Rub the chicken pieces with the salt and pepper.
2. Place the chicken in a glass dish, top with the garlic and thyme, and cover with plastic wrap.

3. Refrigerate for 24 hours.
4. Preheat your oven to 225°F.
5. Rinse the chicken well and pat it dry.
6. In a Dutch oven, melt the fat over low heat.
7. Submerge the chicken in the melted fat.
8. Cook for 2-3 hours, or until the chicken is very tender.
9. To store, place the chicken in a crock or a jar and cover it with the fat.

*Notes: You can use the leftover fat to roast potatoes or vegetables.*

## RECIPE: POTTED BEEF

This is a simple and hearty dish that is perfect for a cold winter's day. It's a great way to use a tougher cut of beef, like a chuck roast, and the result is a tender, flavorful meat that is wonderful served over noodles or mashed potatoes.

### Ingredients:

- 3-pound beef chuck roast, cut into 1-inch cubes
- 1/4 cup of all-purpose flour
- 2 tablespoons of salt
- 1 tablespoon of black pepper
- 2 tablespoons of butter
- 1 onion, chopped
- 2 carrots, chopped
- 2 celery stalks, chopped
- 2 cups of beef broth
- 1 cup of rendered beef tallow or lard

### Instructions:

1. In a bowl, mix together the flour, salt, and pepper.
2. Toss the beef cubes in the flour mixture.
3. In a large pot, melt the butter over medium-high heat.
4. Brown the beef cubes in the butter.
5. Add the onion, carrots, and celery to the pot and cook until softened.
6. Add the beef broth and bring to a simmer.
7. Reduce the heat to low, cover, and cook for 2-3 hours, or until the beef is very tender.
8. Pack the beef and vegetables into a crock or a jar and pour the rendered tallow or lard over it.

*Notes: This is a great dish to make ahead of time. The flavor will only get better with time.*

## RECIPE: RABBIT CONFIT

Rabbit is a lean and delicate meat that is perfect for confit. The slow cooking process makes the meat incredibly tender and flavorful. This is a simple and elegant dish that is sure to impress.

**Ingredients:**

- 1 whole rabbit, cut into 6-8 pieces
- 1/4 cup of kosher salt
- 1 tablespoon of black pepper
- 4 cloves of garlic, smashed
- 4 sprigs of fresh thyme
- 4 cups of rendered lard or tallow

**Instructions:**

1. Rub the rabbit pieces with the salt and pepper.
2. Place the rabbit in a glass dish, top with the garlic and thyme, and cover with plastic wrap.
3. Refrigerate for 24 hours.
4. Preheat your oven to 225°F.
5. Rinse the rabbit well and pat it dry.
6. In a Dutch oven, melt the fat over low heat.
7. Submerge the rabbit in the melted fat.
8. Cook for 2-3 hours, or until the rabbit is very tender.
9. To store, place the rabbit in a crock or a jar and cover it with the fat.

*Notes: You can use the leftover fat to roast potatoes or vegetables.*

### RECIPE: TURKEY CONFIT

This is a wonderful way to preserve a turkey, and it's a great alternative to roasting a whole bird. The meat is incredibly moist and flavorful, and it's perfect for a holiday meal or a special occasion. I like to serve it with a simple cranberry sauce and some wild rice.

**Ingredients:**

- 4 turkey thighs
- 1/4 cup of kosher salt
- 1 tablespoon of black pepper
- 4 cloves of garlic, smashed
- 4 sprigs of fresh sage
- 4 cups of rendered turkey fat, lard, or tallow

**Instructions:**

1. Rub the turkey thighs with the salt and pepper.
2. Place the turkey in a glass dish, top with the garlic and sage, and cover with plastic wrap.
3. Refrigerate for 24 hours.
4. Preheat your oven to 225°F.
5. Rinse the turkey well and pat it dry.
6. In a Dutch oven, melt the fat over low heat.
7. Submerge the turkey in the melted fat.

8. Cook for 3-4 hours, or until the turkey is very tender.
9. To store, place the turkey in a crock or a jar and cover it with the fat.

*Notes: You can use the leftover fat to make a delicious gravy.*

## RECIPE: GOOSE CONFIT

Goose is a rich and flavorful bird that is perfect for confit. The slow cooking process makes the meat incredibly tender and succulent. This is a traditional dish that is often served at Christmas in our community. It's a real treat.

**Ingredients:**

- 4 goose legs
- 1/4 cup of kosher salt
- 1 tablespoon of black pepper
- 4 cloves of garlic, smashed
- 4 sprigs of fresh rosemary
- 4 cups of rendered goose fat, lard, or tallow

**Instructions:**

1. Rub the goose legs with the salt and pepper.
2. Place the goose in a glass dish, top with the garlic and rosemary, and cover with plastic wrap.
3. Refrigerate for 24 hours.
4. Preheat your oven to 225°F.
5. Rinse the goose well and pat it dry.
6. In a Dutch oven, melt the fat over low heat.
7. Submerge the goose in the melted fat.
8. Cook for 3-4 hours, or until the goose is very tender.
9. To store, place the goose in a crock or a jar and cover it with the fat.

*Notes: Goose fat is a prized ingredient in our community. We use it for everything from roasting potatoes to making pastries.*

## RECIPE: POTTED SHRIMP

This is a simple and elegant dish that is perfect for a special occasion. It's a wonderful way to preserve fresh shrimp, and the result is a delicious and flavorful spread that is perfect for serving on crackers or toast points. This is a taste of the sea that you can enjoy any time of year.

**Ingredients:**

- 1 pound of cooked, peeled shrimp
- 1/2 cup of butter, melted
- 1/4 teaspoon of nutmeg
- 1/4 teaspoon of cayenne pepper
- Salt and pepper to taste

**Instructions:**

1. Chop the shrimp into small pieces.
2. In a bowl, mix together the shrimp, butter, nutmeg, and cayenne pepper.
3. Season with salt and pepper to taste.
4. Pack the shrimp mixture into a small crock or a jar.
5. Pour a thin layer of melted butter over the top to seal it.
6. Refrigerate for at least 4 hours, or until the butter is firm.

*Notes: Potted shrimp will keep in the refrigerator for up to a week.*

## RECIPE: POTTED SALMON

This is another wonderful way to preserve fish. It's a simple and delicious spread that is perfect for a light lunch or a tea party. I like to serve it on cucumber slices for a refreshing and elegant treat.

**Ingredients:**

- 1 pound of cooked salmon, flaked
- 1/2 cup of butter, melted
- 1 tablespoon of lemon juice
- 1 tablespoon of fresh dill, chopped
- Salt and pepper to taste

**Instructions:**

1. In a bowl, mix together the salmon, butter, lemon juice, and dill.
2. Season with salt and pepper to taste.
3. Pack the salmon mixture into a small crock or a jar.
4. Pour a thin layer of melted butter over the top to seal it.
5. Refrigerate for at least 4 hours, or until the butter is firm.

*Notes: Potted salmon will keep in the refrigerator for up to a week.*

## RECIPE: RENDERED LARD AND TALLOW

This is not so much a recipe as it is a basic technique that is essential for fat preservation. Rendering your own lard and tallow is a simple and economical way to get a high-quality fat for preserving and cooking. It's a skill that has been passed down through generations in my family, and it's one that I'm proud to share with you.

**Ingredients:**

- Pork fatback or beef suet

**Instructions:**

1. Chop the fat into small pieces.

2. Place the fat in a heavy-bottomed pot over low heat.
3. Cook slowly, stirring occasionally, until the fat has melted and the solid pieces have turned brown and crispy. These crispy pieces are called cracklings, and they are a delicious snack.
4. Strain the liquid fat through a piece of cheesecloth to remove the cracklings and any other solids.
5. Pour the liquid fat into clean jars and let it cool completely.

*Notes: Rendered lard and tallow will keep for months in a cool, dark place. You can use it for preserving meat, for cooking, or for making soap.*

## QUICK FAT PRESERVATION RECIPES – AMISH POTTED MEATS & CONFITS

| Recipe Name | Main Ingredients | Instructions (Condensed) | Notes & Serving Ideas |
|---|---|---|---|
| Potted Pork | Cooked pork shoulder, rendered lard, salt, pepper | Shred warm meat, season, pack into crocks, cover with melted lard. Cool and store. | Keeps 3+ months in a cool cellar. Serve on bread or biscuits. |
| Duck Confit (Amish-Style) | Duck legs, salt, thyme, garlic, rendered duck fat | Salt overnight, rinse, cook slowly submerged in fat 3 hrs, pack under fat. | Tender, flavorful, and long-keeping. |
| Potted Beef with Herbs | Cooked roast beef, tallow or suet, thyme, pepper | Shred beef, season, press into jars, pour hot tallow to cover. | Spreadable beef for biscuits or sandwiches. |
| Goose Rillettes | Goose meat, garlic, salt, rendered goose fat | Simmer shredded meat with fat and garlic until paste-like; pack under fat. | A holiday delicacy in many Amish homes. |
| Potted Chicken with Sage | Shredded cooked chicken, butter, sage, salt | Blend meat and herbs, cover with melted butter or lard, seal tight. | Smooth and savory; excellent for tea sandwiches. |
| Lard-Sealed Sausage Patties | Cooked sausage patties, rendered lard | Fry patties lightly, cool, pack into crock, cover with melted lard. | Traditional winter breakfast meat. |
| Beef Confit in Tallow | Cubed cooked beef, tallow, black pepper, bay leaf | Cook beef slowly in tallow, then pack and submerge completely in fat. | Keeps several months in cold storage. |
| Turkey Pâté in Fat | Cooked turkey, herbs, butter, salt | Blend turkey fine, season, press into jars, pour melted butter to seal. | Spread on toast or crackers. |
| Rabbit Confit with Juniper | Rabbit pieces, salt, juniper berries, lard | Salt overnight, rinse, cook low in lard 2–3 hrs, pack under fat. | Mild game flavor, tender texture. |

| Recipe Name | Main Ingredients | Instructions (Condensed) | Notes & Serving Ideas |
|---|---|---|---|
| Ham Ends in Fat | Diced ham, lard or bacon grease | Warm ham gently, pour melted fat over to cover completely. Cool sealed. | Great for beans, eggs, or quick gravies. |

## Storage & Safety Notes

- **Temperature:** Store sealed pots or jars in a **cool, dark cellar (below 50°F)** or refrigerated for longer life.
- **Fat Seal:** Always ensure the fat layer completely covers meat with **no air pockets.**
- **Shelf Life:** 3–6 months cool stored, 8–12 months refrigerated.
- **Use Tip:** Once opened, keep refrigerated and use within 1–2 weeks.

# CHAPTER 7: BUILDING YOUR PRESERVATION SYSTEM

As we've journeyed together through these pages, I've shared with you the five pillars of meat preservation that have sustained my family for generations. We've explored the modern convenience of pressure canning, the ancient art of salt curing, the fragrant magic of smoking, the elemental simplicity of drying, and the forgotten wisdom of fat preservation. Each of these methods is a powerful tool in its own right, but the true secret to a well-stocked pantry lies in learning how to weave them together into a complete preservation system.

In my childhood home, preservation wasn't a once-a-year event; it was a way of life. It was a constant rhythm of activity that ebbed and flowed with the seasons. In the fall, when the hogs were butchered, the hams and bacons were put up in salt, the sausages were hung in the smokehouse, and the lard was rendered for potted meat. In the summer, when the garden was overflowing, the pressure canner was working overtime, preserving vegetables and meats for the lean winter months. And throughout the year, there was always a batch of jerky being made or a crock of something delicious bubbling away in a cool corner of the cellar.

This is the beauty of a preservation system. It's not about choosing one method over another; it's about using the right method for the right food at the right time. It's about creating a pantry that is not just full, but also diverse, with a wide variety of foods that will nourish your family and delight your taste buds.

## *THE PANTRY PRINCIPLE: FIRST IN, FIRST OUT*

One of the most important principles of a good preservation system is the "first in, first out" rule. This simply means that you should always use the oldest foods in your pantry first. This ensures that nothing goes to waste and that your food is always at its peak of freshness.

To practice this principle, it's important to label everything you preserve with the date it was made. When you're putting away a new batch of canned goods or a freshly smoked ham, be sure to place it behind the older items on the shelf. This way, you'll always be reaching for the oldest food first.

## COMBINING METHODS FOR MAXIMUM FLAVOR AND SHELF LIFE

Some of the most delicious and long-lasting preserved meats are made by combining two or more preservation methods. For example, a traditional country ham is first cured in salt, then smoked, and then air-dried for months, or even years. The result is a ham with a depth of flavor that is simply unparalleled.

Another example is the smoked sausage we made in Chapter 4. These sausages are first cured with salt and spices, then smoked, and then they can be air-dried for a more traditional cured sausage. The combination of curing and smoking gives the sausage a wonderful flavor and a long shelf life.

Don't be afraid to experiment with combining methods. You might be surprised at the delicious results you can achieve.

## A WORD ON FERMENTED SAUSAGES

As you become more confident in your preservation skills, you may want to try your hand at making fermented sausages, like salami or pepperoni. These are some of the most delicious and shelf-stable of all the preserved meats, but they are also the most challenging to make. They require a deep understanding of the curing process and a carefully controlled environment for drying.

I haven't included any recipes for fermented sausages in this book because they are an advanced technique that is not for the beginner. But I encourage you to seek out more information on this fascinating topic as you continue on your preservation journey. It's a rewarding skill that will take your charcuterie to the next level.

## CONCLUSION: A BLESSING FOR YOUR HANDS AND YOUR HOME

We've come to the end of our journey together, but in many ways, your journey is just beginning. The skills I've shared with you in this book are more than just a collection of recipes; they are a connection to our past and a key to our future. They are a way to nourish our families, to build community, and to live a more self-reliant and sustainable life.

I hope that as you begin to practice these old ways, you will feel a sense of connection to the generations of women who have stood in their kitchens, just as you are standing in yours, preserving the bounty of the earth for their loved ones. I hope you will feel the satisfaction of a pantry filled with the fruits of your labor, and the peace of mind that comes from knowing you can provide for your family, no matter what the future may hold.

And so, I leave you with a blessing, the same blessing that my grandmother whispered over my hands as she taught me to knead bread and to snap beans. May your hands be blessed with skill and your heart be filled with gratitude. May your pantry be full and your home be a place of warmth and abundance. And may you always walk in the simple, humble way of our ancestors, with faith in God and a deep respect for the good earth He has given us.

# APPENDICES

## Appendix A: Meat Preservation Method Comparison Chart

| Method | Best For | Shelf Life | Skill Level | Equipment Needed |
|--------|----------|------------|-------------|------------------|
| Pressure Canning | Soups, stews, meats in broth | 1-2 years | Intermediate | Pressure canner, jars, lids |
| Salt Curing | Ham, bacon, corned beef | Months to years | Intermediate | Curing salts, food-grade container |
| Smoking | Sausage, fish, poultry, ham | Weeks to months | Beginner to Intermediate | Smoker or grill, wood chips |
| Drying & Pemmican | Jerky, biltong, pemmican | Months to decades | Beginner to Intermediate | Dehydrator or oven, grinder |
| Fat Preservation | Confit, potted meats, rillettes | Months | Intermediate | Crock or jars, rendered fat |

## Appendix B: Curing Salt Guide

| Curing Salt | Composition | Use | Notes |
|-------------|-------------|-----|-------|
| Pink Salt #1 | 6.25% sodium nitrite, 93.75% sodium chloride | Curing meats that will be cooked, such as bacon, ham, and corned beef. | Also known as Prague Powder #1 or Insta Cure #1. Not to be confused with Himalayan pink salt. |
| Pink Salt #2 | 6.25% sodium nitrite, 4% sodium nitrate, 89.75% sodium chloride | Curing meats that will be air-dried for a long time, such as salami, pepperoni, and country ham. | Also known as Prague Powder #2 or Insta Cure #2. The sodium nitrate breaks down into sodium nitrite over time, providing a long-term cure. |

*Important: Curing salts are not table salt and should be used in very small, precise amounts. Always follow the recipe carefully when using curing salts.*

## APPENDIX C: WOOD SMOKING FLAVOR PROFILE CHART

| Wood | Flavor Profile | Best With | Notes |
|---|---|---|---|
| Hickory | Strong, bacon-like | Pork, beef | The classic smoking wood. |
| Apple | Mild, sweet, fruity | Poultry, pork | A great all-purpose smoking wood. |
| Mesquite | Strong, earthy | Beef, dark meats | Can be overpowering if used too much. |
| Alder | Delicate, slightly sweet | Salmon, fish | The traditional wood for smoking salmon. |
| Oak | Medium, smoky | Beef, lamb, brisket | A good all-purpose smoking wood. |
| Cherry | Mild, sweet, fruity | Poultry, pork, beef | Gives meat a beautiful reddish color. |
| Pecan | Mild, nutty, sweet | Poultry, pork | A good alternative to hickory. |